I am
Abigail Adams

adapted by Gabriella DeGennaro

PENGUIN YOUNG READERS LICENSES
An Imprint of Penguin Random House LLC, New York

Published in 2021 by Penguin Young Readers Licenses, an imprint of Penguin Random House LLC, New York. Manufactured in China.

Visit us online at www.penguinrandomhouse.com.

ISBN 9780593222164   10 9 8 7 6 5 4 3 2 1

"What do you think of my sweet yo-yo moves?" Xavier called out to his sister, Yadina, as he twirled a yo-yo through the air with style.

"They're *yo* good," she giggled. "Just like this picture I'm going to paint for Mom's birthday."

"Ooh, your mom is going to love that!" Brad cheered.

Yadina sat at the craft table in the museum looking at her paint-by-numbers kit. She was just about ready to paint some gorgeous green hills onto the canvas.

"Oh no! This is a disaster!" Yadina shouted. Inside the kit, the tube of green paint was dried up. "Now I can't do Mom's painting," she said.

"Don't worry, Yadina. I know how to solve your problem,"
Xavier said.

Yadina knew exactly what he was going to say.

"To the Secret Museum!" they both cheered, racing off down the
hall excitedly.

"Of course," Brad sighed as he ran to catch up with them.

Once inside the Secret Museum, they found a ribbon on the podium.

"What's a ribbon got to do with not having a *very* important color? It's not even green!" exclaimed Yadina.

Just then, an image of Abigail Adams appeared.

"I wonder how she can help with my mom's present," Yadina said.

"There's only one way to find out," said Xavier. "Ready for adventure?"

With a great burst of light, the friends traveled back in time to Massachusetts in 1754.

"Look—a dollhouse!" Yadina shouted, and rushed over to get a better look.

The dollhouse was old and shabby, but that didn't stop Yadina and Dr. Zoom from exploring. Giggling, she pushed Dr. Zoom through the door of the tiny house, but when she tried to wiggle him back out, the walls collapsed!

"Oh, that silly old dollhouse," said a voice. "It's always falling apart!"

"It's her! It's Abigail Adams," Xavier whispered to his friends.

"My friend John was going to lend me his hammer and nails to fix it, but he's always busy," Abigail said. "We can fix it ourselves!" she added enthusiastically.

Xavier was confused. "But if you don't have a hammer and nails, how are you going to fix it?"

"We just have to be resourceful!" Abigail said. "That means using whatever you *do* have."

They all began hunting around the yard for something they could use to fix the house.

After a little while, Yadina felt discouraged. She had been searching all over the yard and hadn't found a hammer or nails.

"This is hopeless . . . just like my painting. I've only found a flower, a watering can, and some ribbons," she cried. "We can't use any of this stuff to fix a dollhouse."

"Did you say ribbons?" Abigail said. "That's it!" The friends watched curiously as Abigail wove the ribbons into a braid. "We can use this to tie the dollhouse pieces together! We can use my hair ribbon, too!"

"Whoa," Xavier said, amazed. "Who knew ribbons were so handy?"

The friends worked together to braid the ribbons as strong as rope. With one final twist, the house was fixed!

Yadina turned to her friends. "Abigail sure is good at doing a lot with what she's got! I wonder what else she can do."

"Looks like we're about to find out," added Xavier as Berby appeared, glowing bright.

In a flash of light, they time-traveled again—this time to an attic in 1775.

"Where are we?" Yadina asked.

Suddenly, Abigail Adams entered carrying a large pile of straw, and there was a tired soldier behind her.

"There may not be any bedrooms left," she said to the soldier, "but we can do a lot with what we've got." She shaped the straw into a bed on the floor and covered him with a coat as if it were a blanket. When she looked up, Abigail noticed the three friends.

"I'm glad you're here! I could really use your help! Follow me," she said as they went down the stairs.

Downstairs, Xavier, Yadina, and Brad were surprised to find the house filled with other soldiers and many of Abigail's neighbors in need of help.

"What's going on?" Xavier asked.

"For the last fifteen years, the people have been told what to do by another country," Abigail told them. "But now, we want to be our *own* country. It's a revolution!"

"A revolution?" Brad asked.

"The American Revolution," explained Yadina. "It's when the United States becomes its very own country."

"Building a country is hard work," continued Abigail. "Sometimes there isn't enough food or shelter to go around."

"Well, you've got us here to help." Yadina beamed.

The friends worked quickly and helped people find a place to sit
and rest and eat. Just when things were running smoothly, Xavier
and Brad rushed up to Yadina in a panic.

"We're out of places for people to sit!" Xavier cried.

"And we're out of bowls for soup. *And* spoons!" Brad added. "What do we do?"

"We just have to be resourceful," Yadina said, determined.

She spotted some barrels in the corner of the room. "We can use these as chairs," she suggested.

Her eyes continued to search around the room until she found a cupboard with stacks of cups. "And people can drink the soup from cups!" she added.

"Very resourceful, Yadina," Abigail said proudly.

The friends continued to work together until everyone was fed and seated comfortably.

"Abigail Adams did so much to help people," Brad said admiringly.

"And if Abigail can do all this, then I bet I can paint that picture for Mom with the colors I have," Yadina said. She thanked Abigail and turned to her friends. She was ready to go home.

A moment later, they were back in the museum. Yadina was ready to tackle her painting kit!

As she practiced her brushstrokes, alternating from yellow to blue, she brushed a bit of blue paint over some yellow.

"Hold up," she said, staring at the colors on her paint plate. "Blue and yellow make *green*!"

Thrilled, she continued painting—creating just the right shades of green with yellow and blue.

"Ta-da!" cheered Yadina as she presented her finished painting to her friends.

"Nice work, Yadina!" Brad said.

"And now for the best part!" Yadina said.

Yadina called out to her mom and rushed over to her with the painting.

"I think she likes it," Xavier observed, watching his sister grin from ear to ear as their mother pulled her into a big hug.